MW01519113

IN/SOMNIA

Library of Congress Cataloging-in-Publications Data

Adnan, Etel
    In/somnia / Etel Adnan.
        p. cm.
    ISBN 0-942996-48-8 (acid-free paper)
    I. Title: Insomnia. II. Title

PS3551.D65I57 2002
813'.54--dc21

                                                    2002193080

The Post-Apollo Press
35 Marie Street
Sausalito, California 94965

Cover drawing and book design by Simone Fattal

Printed in the United States of America on acid-free paper

Etel Adnan

In/somnia

THE POST-APOLLO PRESS

ACKNOWLEDGEMENTS

Some sections of *In/somnia* have appeared in *Technologies of Measure: A Celebration of Bay Area Writers, Rooms* and *Banipal.*

IN/SOMNIA

I

1. Trees. Threes. In green/gray
   splash/noise. Hoe in garden.
   Rose in lock/ed room

2. Shine with chair &
   in/som/nia radio stupid
   stupid/ly chance clusters
   Of temperatures. traffic
   and weather to/gether

3. auto-making sprink-ling
   over flower/ed cab/bage
   stooooory weeks before
   an airport

4. silver-car. waves.
   relating to pro
   testing. fear. shots.
   as many kisses

5. twelve (+one).morning.
   mostly/horizontal/matter
   hates. Bay impersonal
   mobil-mobilized by (bye)
   money. Incurable propositions.

6. Afternoon. a bench. Phone.
   Hills chasing bills.Baby–
   otters. dark soprano. ***
   solar disrupted. when

II

1. Pills by lamp. sheets.
    shut car by kitchen.
    Ap/ap/appropriation of.
    A finger un/till november

2. walk by/Pacific. overflow
    of. of/thoughts in reservoirs
    of expectation. blue eyes.
    stand. in mirror

3. lack of money/root.zigzaging
    in Lethe. Not leaving.

4. coins & stars have light
    in common. Purple come/ons!
    Sorrow on lateral... panes.
    deep. deepness.

5. Only aboard a question.
    army red/ready. for the
    curb of an elbow. cut-in
    to silence while ...

III

1. Feever. Feet on bath/
   bar/room. Bottle's
   reBellion. boxes filled
   wt/predatory shells.
   line

2. Al/ways + never/the/less
   = not/wtih/standing..
   tea.

3. not a concern. usually
   used. heavy-door-metal
   queen spat on snow.

4. sweating dream of forms.
   silvery machine for, for
   perversion. three

5. play lute for clue
   dark/ness re/lated to
   air. chimney un-swapped.
   parallel love-affair

IV

1. spinning condolences – to
   thistles. wooooooooo
   obsolete thoughts. rumors
   of surrender . under

2. cold verticality. rectan-
   gular weather's canyons.
   a range of incertitude
   *** move/ing

3. double/question conceals
   (wet) weapons stockmarket
   of oblivion altered to
   ease

4. deliberate land fascination
   lighter light side to the
   ocean destined... buttons
   & belts

5. body for transient sale.
   .... apprehension
   among daffodils. Copper
   of why and where

6. sub(marine)division for
   trouble slow/ly sole/ly
   of annihilation. time
   comes hard. sky torn
   membrane.

7. swindle weather assets.
   furor double-lying on
   merger.

V

1. positioning errancy. zinc
    and flags panick about
    past/seminars

2. ominous metaphors cemetering
    piling dirt on spirit free
    & departuring to gassing
    tanks

3. Eat it ? on the road 2
    notebooks of traces +
    morphine – there/

4. matinees of shoes turning
    at eye-level of swelling
    opportunities... brrrr

5. bid on bindery when
    (glass) through travels
    epileptic blueberries.

VI

1. Follow signs. *** cliffs of
   un/belief. considering actuality
   of being live.

2. .Laird sprawls unsaying.
   trapped on ranch w/view
   on lake. & wuthering realities
   at gang-speed fall for pollen

3. through transparancy. wheels.
   orchards of mushrooms. physical
   & mental brains fuse. hydrogen
   bomb half-human half-airplane.

4. through friendly skies bullet s
   unkind by nature. Ohhhh ill/
   lumination.

5. fencing angel's insanity
   grating winter's smile:
   game of pool.

VII

1. out/side ... fall
    on wall on oh yes!
    black-out end/ing
    sleep slippery tongue –
    ong... ong.

2. winds. on – tight
    where wear 1, 2,
    kling/ling pleese help

3. there loss the/re sky
    motet loss.of. what
    was / ache? . hooooo

4. what? Satan/sa/———> huh
    ho/mo/sap...
    huh. Great/breath
    brease. ziz zee O Khu

5. End———>less night
    let's
    WHY no not/nothin
    bad. Dead SUN. W/here?

VIII

1. Hou – ou ouh we
    See... whab... of...
    slipping –   – slip
    hell!   no help
    this.   stupidly hour

2. in/tense/in/season
    who? ——⟶ whooooo when?
    how?   how – ever. who
    bears this bull
    sit/sitting/in/curriculums
    of loss/——⟶ heads/head
    gGoOnNeE

3. now/once/——/flatness
    zooming   in   non
    /visibility
    pulled/out/the pull/of
    sea's pull   to be new/... xxxx
    never & now — pills –
    on – where? ——⟶ fffffff

10

IX

1. fasting on absence.
   wedwedding air. linen
   bedbedding . ink-rain

2. motion(less) rivers
   riveting meadows of
   want. red cube penetrated
   by (with) agony

3. dessicated by thirst
   kid/ding! tuned to
   meesery tunnel Minotaur
   hushhushy in wee hours
   Completion

4. Errand beast/night/
   ly. visible. monster.
   moon loon broom

5. color gone. Kurtains
   thththink about.t.tit

6. Pale. dear/est hamlet
   heimat. winding/wind/

widow/somber obscu-
tity. avalance like
lack-of-dream. noise

X

for Bob Grenier

1. Through. imaging.
    mountains even.
    water eyes shut.

2. mirror, boxed-in/
    production of one's
    light. (lightly)
    truck/load of. sweet
    night/mare with
    Faust.

3. trees on fables.
    legs parting
    on linen. on hold.
    Nebulous.love. of
    thoughts

4. tiniest of visions
    an———— gelic. fever.
    gulch. O C.a.l.i.f.o.r.n.i.a.!
            Dimensions

5.   blurs. o no! not hiding
       mild. wild. kind.
       hind... fatigue leads
       ahead. ???????

6.   split   cloud
       crooked effervescence
       height of passing
       hour . un(yielding.)

7.   the re/turn/rerun
       lived-in devil
       a throw of
       res/s/urgence.
       ex/haustion

8.   his/owl/on/
       the/ridge.
       uuuuuuuh!

XI

1. Ir/reversibly clarity
    over and why. stairs .
    whales eat elephant/
    ear. when tears marry.
    to sea. the middle's
    middle in/som/nia

2. women envy sailors
    for additional distrac-
    tion. never colored.
    the police stand

3. on a cycleByecycle. Auto
    nomous fear(roofs) the
    wind's hunger for repetition.
    two lines at a time

4. Funeral/s on 2 feet
    to carry on one's
    back. Trans/parency
    of single mind. Dis-
    placement – care/fully –
    of.a.sentence.

5. Bodies fuse fragility
   with marrows. Plus
   Plus fanfare. napkins
   are maps. no food maternal
   traffic blocks desire
   on asphalt —

XII

1. foam of Red Sea. Cat/ching
   Mercury, Lord of Time.
   visiting this room (?).
   Passage to: no/where
   fire's proportions

2. sun, moon, free
   what's ... sleep?!
   ooooo! booooo. Hourly
   eyes.reversed. ***

3. lion. judgment of .
   indistinct/ness. Red
   with/in black/ness. O
   non/certitutde of non/
   existence. The/re.

4. Break:up. down. over.
   through. So on and on
   until morning breaks.
   in. Ever.

XIII

1. ranger's in/un/certitude
   for danger/ous oaks.
   odd numbers are odd
   in rect/angular weather's
   melting

2. light in mental
   ??? metal ??? brainy
   vision become lit
   river.

3. 4 wheels take you.
   to xxx over/pass.
   centaurs on all
   four. for klarity's
   sake. distinctions.

4. flying partly sunny,
   apparition. what is it? this
   is wet.
   wet. wetly deltafish

XIV

1. a pizza's   theology
    theos. ouranos. in San
    Andreas' counter-clock.
    xxxxxxxxxxxxxxxxxx
    crooked str-strategies
    make op/timal op/tions

2. apple/tree/cherry/or
    klear   creek   search/ed/
    seer   seeing   there!
    come   comet   coming
    plane/planets/drifting

3. hou!   hou!   hot!   hot!
    quick.   windows, wind
    wind/in/fast   vast
    leenen

4. capsizing   over   horizon
    of luck.   to the morrow.
    they say. where's relief?

5. meandering   through
    one's memory.

XV

1. tools. Why
    any/thing? Where?
    Pressure. Precious.
    Get/ting a sting on
    a fool

2. Angles on all four.
    Ret(dis)tribution
    one + one + 2 + 2
    puts one (two) to
    sleep. Not. Yet.
    Not. may it be.

3. Diff ficulty breath/
    breathing. Schpitt.
    fewer hot spellings.
    Climb.you.monsters.

4. Mor.mapp.yes.maps.
    Yesses/yup: tools –
    for dying. night
    plus nights. Not
    yet

5. while it lasts

XVI

1. aperturic / fever
   noises. night's
   end/less beauty/fully
   race, run run oh boy!
   sleep's run away
   ex/plosion / doors

2. im/patience pa/tient
   sand clock tic/ticking
   8 Ham/let/king/go!

3. demain lest where? socks
   in forest by dementia
   ordered. Lucia beach
   free skreaming in there

4. celibaby cell tell Queeg
   Gone the mouse the catt
   the queeg when you're
   borred... say! say!

5. sun   moon frrreee hou ou!
   damn it damn it un/catch
   gone gone shut heat on
   pillow's end ... well. the
   uncoming.

XVII

1. wings   from   one's   late
    o minous voyage.
    (pestilence) ô
    half $^1/2$ have moon
    mind & number

2. healed mansions of ...
    everybody's fate
    in the balance ... in
    xeroxed   (blank)
    sheets   shh

3. drugs for en/light/n/ment
    of THE fright/e/ned
    un/stable —
    .   to start. warranting.
    the (?) night.

4. sulfur:
    holding re/surrected
    baby. in arms.
    arms.

XVIII

1. altered epi/fanny. zzzz
    nerves — neurves. leaves
    in symmetry. for dorrmant
    lady in lace. in diamond

2. now transient horizon-
    tal life. Buttes. slough.
    (slow, low) over ...
    ?????

3. warm warmth speech
    between eagles and
    and (!) the poor (pour)
    vi.si.bi.li.ty. ...
    of somber desires ...
    w w w w w w w w w

4. maligNancy taken off
    time's isolation. off
    rain/bows

5. At the bone. up
    there.

XIX

1. Night falling. again. Not again.
   long/line no help help/less
   terror stop the terr...
   terribly all over/ over
   what?

2. blows bellowing blowing
   paper and doors and what
   else? Is is it? is it coming?
   Yes. time. Last time

3. lasting timing ever-ever
   snoring orderal or deal
   dealer of cards   of smoke
   tick/ no no end

4. shhh – weee – buzzz
   buzing pele-mele
   keep   held hold-it! keep
   insane in/sane the right
   to wait wait! waited for
   for wait a minute for/the/
   dark/light of morning

5. collapsibles

XX

1. Aeschylus nothing
   nihil ist cloud-bearing
   battle stoop/lie on
   ground welll

2. steam-boat where's Greece?
   the object ab/ject. Pan the god
   ear/ful of space

3. thru   turn.   pull up
   cacophonus – phone –
   (messages) cross that
               measure – until
   the garden's rise ///

4. suspension: longer than...
   is usual. usually. penetrate
   push/in stay/there in
   obscured korridor – door –
   dors – till the heart
   (of the matter) gives up
   up _____ there.

5. ubiquitous is
       night/ness
   dead is ????????? on
   couch ::::::: lust extinction
   extinct   breathing
   thing of leaves,
   of Kalendar's last
   last/ing ...

XXI

1. Bye & bye gentle meta-
   phoros. Go to _____ your _____
   grave. Pillars. stand/ing
   matelas/s/s ...... no! _____ no!

2. go/going   a.way.
   way out. out/there.
   where we were . where?
   stu/por /stu/pid/ly/

3. memory of first
   life/ + me.mo.ry. of
   pre/sent − a gift − a
   light. jugger/naut
   keep out

4. secret   secret/ions of
   things.   metallic. past.
   ressur/gence resurrect
   from. red eggs. balls.
   rope. hang man hangs
   /slippery/sleep. over.
   on this cover/up.

5. Eluding / eva.nescence/
nativitiy.of.lion.crouching.
coughing.cough.ingenious/
ly.on.elongated (at gate) of
body

XXII

1. No clouds in this room
    but... (?)   mountain–
    blanket... blank .
    vibrations underneath
    neathhhhhhhhhhhhhhh

2. to the muffled bells
    La Belle ****
    casual ties ... shit!
    casualties... cock/
    roaches... partout

3. that's nocturnal
    night/ly horror
    terror ter... O(ooo)h!

4. never say mine
    ear. sand of sediments
    rem/nants /of/ memory
    mory mory ry ry

XXIII

1. weather & war live to gether.
    off black lilies. spider
    & Spicer... and Kyger
    waou! im, im-possible
    descent dissent

2. err err in loved black-
    berries. Hunger in middle
    existence. who's calling?

3. snow full/train like
    ach... captive to day's
    end. burly dream/ing

4. charkoal chh shh, „,
    deversoir der die das
    maps ***** sliding

5. non/stop argument,
    with ...
    inter(mittent)nationes
    1 2 3 4 mosquitos gate
    gates

XXIV

1. hallucinated visions of
the sea. see see! time/
table for the waiting.

2. 5-stars prisons for
Af(ter)ghanistan. bullish
bullet   bulletins –
bulldozing blood of
curling l.i.b.e.r.a.t.o.r.s.

3. Please, angel, come
in mess & messenger
of messes missing
the treason

4. how to bear this in/tense
this: love of thought,
abysmal. abolition.

XXV

1. once, once every second.
    implosion of inner
    press/ure on press/ure.

2. something does me.
    counting the hours/
    with the dead. houuuuu
    dressed-up, the wind
    (wel)comes in and around

3. sirens are angry abstrac-
    tions suc/king my sleep
    sleeping options. fleas'
    blood.

4. pillows.of.stones.of.
    thorns.of.wet.praying
    sshh sshh the faucet.
    la potence for your's
    ... your queendo(o)m.

XXVI

1. Frights turn. as they
   turn when birds (then)
   unfly their winggy
   wings.

2. drink before. and
   after the sound

3. territorial haggard T.V.
   Klosed. Keeps language
   of (?) of scissors.
   Progressing procession
   . the Spirit.

4. eyes never blue when
   shut. become screams
   and screens. Don't call
   him: Ishmael.

XXVII

1. divide/rs all walls
    mem/brains soft /
    harsh   fuff fluff ff
    deep/fry ooze

2. bundled/up/limbs
    eat before the
    fore of keeled
    kneeled animal
    anima mundane

3. mind-set vaporated
    old buddy, hey,
    in ... chaos   not in
    nothing/ness

4. wild nights of
    non-mobility
    mobile sleep
    going gone in (?)
    in   in
    an Old.olds.mobile
    /squeezed. in.vein.